CREATIVE WAYS TO LOVE & ENCOURAGE HER

JEFFERSON BETHKE

Published in Kihei, HI, by Bethke Writings. Bethke Writings titles may be purchased in bulk for educational, business, fund-raising or sales promotional use. For information, please e-mail info@bethkewritings.com.

Unless otherwise noted, scriptures are taken from the Holy Bible, New International Version®,NIV®. Copyright © 1973, 1978, 1984, 2011 by Biblica, Inc.™ Used by permission of Zondervan. All rights reserved worldwide. www.zondervan.com.

The Library of Congress Cataloging-in-Publication
Data is on file with the Library of Congress
ISBN-13: 978-0692720363

TABLE OF CONTENTS

HOW TO GET THE MOST OUT OF THIS BOOK.

First off, you rock. By getting these paired books and wanting to go through them with your significant other, you obviously are already dominating at life! We have prayed over this project and really believe it can be a fun way to cultivate a healthy relationship and bring back the joy and intimacy that sometimes gets lost amidst the every day activities.

To get the most out of this book, we'd first say lean in. Lean into the ideas, the spontaneity and the parts that stretch you the most. Don't be afraid to just go for it, have fun and create memories. We are firm believers that with these two books, whatever you put into it you will get out of it (and isn't that true with all our relationships as a whole?). But also know that this is just a template. Some things won't fit for your relationship or you can't do based on certain locations, resources and other variables. We have tried to make every day as applicable for everyone as possible. So with that being said, feel free to morph it, change it, adapt it and do whatever you need to do to get the most out of it. Because at the end of the day, the goal isn't to follow this book rigidly and "cross each day off your checklist" but rather it's to bring a fresh vibrancy and life back to your relationship.

Also, a quick note to the dating folks out there. Obviously we are married so we are coming from that perspective. We also wanted to write this so dating couples could have a useful tool! As mentioned above, you might have to morph it in a different way too. When not living together, some of these are a little harder since when you're dating you probably don't see each other every single day. So feel free to stretch this out over a few months or pick a couple per week.

JEFF & ALYSSA BETHKE

DAY ONE: PRAYER

Some of the most encouraging times ever in our marriage is when Alyssa tells me she's praying for me. Not just in general but when she tells me what her prayer was. That she's praying for my walk with Jesus. That I'd come to know Him in a deeper way that day. She prays for my purity. That I'd protect and guard my thoughts and mind. She prays that God would give me wisdom in how to parent. And on. And on.

It makes me feel not alone. It makes me feel like the bad days or the hard days or the days where I feel shame or temptation, I have an advocate. Not only is Alyssa in my corner, but most of all Jesus is. He stands with me and for me.

Make a point to ask your wife or girlfriend how they could use prayer. Then sometime over the next week write a prayer out for them on a card or piece of paper and give it to them. Or today simply ask if you can pray for them out loud.

JOURNAL BELOW:

WRITE WHAT YOU LEARNED TODAY, HOW IT WENT AND WHAT MEMORIES WERE MADE.

DAY TWO: THOUGHTFULNESS

Alyssa and I just had our second child this year (2016). When we were in the hospital, as the dad, you do a good amount of sitting around. I don't know about you but when I sit around I basically just want to eat. Food. Lots of it.

Alyssa could sense this and told me to open her overnight bag. When I looked in it, I saw a few of my favorite snacks (peanut butter M&M's for those wondering). And I immediately felt so loved. Why? Because I was thought of beforehand. It probably took Alyssa 80 cents at the grocery store the week before and about 15 seconds of extra attention. That's all it cost. It was this tiny moment of feeling special and understood, like she knew me. (Well, also because I get hungry, so I guess it was in her best interest to keep me fed too.)

Think of her most favorite treat. Or coffee drink. Surprise her with it. When she asks why? Say, "No reason, I was just thinking of you."

JOURNAL BELOW:

WRITE WHAT YOU LEARNED TODAY, HOW IT WENT AND WHAT MEMORIES WERE MADE.

DAY THREE: LAUGHTER

"Laughter is carbonated holiness."

That's a quote from one of my favorite writers, Anne Lamott. It's true though. There's something about laughter that is downright sacred. When you're laughing, there's joy you can't explain. It does something to you. Warms your heart. Another favorite quote of mine is, "Always laugh when you can. It's cheap medicine." –George Gordon Byron.

It's an understatement to say Alyssa and I love to laugh. I'm always doing something dumb around the house. Making up a song of sorts or talking in these weird accents that I make up. (Frankly, if anyone BUT Alyssa saw these antics, they'd probably think I was crazy.) I've started to realize that laughing is something that connects us. Brings us closer together. Cultivating joy can actually be like a bonding agent in a relationship. It makes the relationship stronger.

Be creative! How can you make your woman laugh today? Maybe it's as simply as reading the jokes on the back of a Laffy Taffy wrapper. (Let's be honest, those are the best anyway.) Or maybe you do some funny dance or antic right after dinner time. Your goal today is make her laugh!

JOURNAL BELOW:

WRITE WHAT YOU LEARNED TODAY, HOW IT WENT AND WHAT MEMORIES WERE MADE.

_____

_____

_____

DAY FOUR: COMMUNICATION

Yesterday Alyssa and I had a little fight. Or...disagreement is probably a better word but you know what I mean. Those times where you're both a little frustrated and you start getting that feeling in your head, "I know I'm right. Why doesn't she blank." You can fill in the blank.

In the disagreement with Alyssa, when I really started to think about it, I realized it actually wasn't because of the reason we were fighting. It was because we didn't properly communicate beforehand. And when you don't communicate, then expectations are not met and that's usually ground zero for tension, strife and more.

A lot of times, the disagreements aren't the actual problem. They are just the symptom. They are showing that something earlier or previous is the real culprit. The real reason why there is frustration.

Ask her how you can communicate better. Ask her if there are any instances or things you say or do that frustrate her. Rehash the past few disagreements and ask how you could have communicated better before they happened in order for it to not happen.

JOURNAL BELOW:

WRITE WHAT YOU LEARNED TODAY, HOW IT WENT AND WHAT MEMORIES WERE MADE.

DAY
FIVE:
DANCE

Alyssa and I are big fans of music always on in the house. We usually turn worship music on in the morning and have it playing in the background through the day. But once it gets to dinner time, especially if I decide to hop in the kitchen and cook, I like to listen to something with a little more funk.

This usually means Taylor Swift, Justin Timberlake, Bruno Mars and maybe some Justin Beiber. (Don't judge me...because I know you're thinking about judging me right now. Is it too late now to say sorry?) And when a good song comes on there's a good chance I'll grab Alyssa and start twirling her, dancing with her and giving her a little old school dip for the grand finale. My favorite part is that Kinsley absolutely loves it and starts giggling the whole time.

There's something about dancing that brings joy and life. So for today, dance with her. It can be a funky spontaneous dinner dance. It can be you turning something on in the car and getting out in the parking lot for a few minutes. It can mean going old school with some Macarena even. Most of all have fun with it, don't be afraid to let loose and dance away!

JOURNAL BELOW:

WRITE WHAT YOU LEARNED TODAY, HOW IT WENT AND WHAT MEMORIES WERE MADE.

DAY SIX: FORGIVE— NESS

Just a few hours ago (from the time I am typing this) Alyssa and I got into one of those little disagreements. You know, the ones where by the time you get to the end of it, you can't really even remember why you were arguing in the first place.

This one definitely was my fault. I had made a dumb side comment that was meant to be funny but in retrospect was just snarky and hurtful. When I made the comment, we were in the grocery store and just about to part ways to conquer and divide our shopping list (the only right way to do it, especially with kids, CAN I GET AN AMEN). It gave me a few minutes to think on it. You know what I realized? It was simply my fault. I was wrong and what I said was hurtful. It was In that moment I felt bad and realized I needed to apologize and ask for forgiveness. A couple minutes later once we reconvened, I said I was sorry. I asked her to forgive me.

Then it hit me—forgiveness truly is one of the sustaining powers of a relationship. Without it, surely every relationship would venture into realms of resentment, hurt, bitterness and more. And that stuff can destroy a relationship. I'd say hands down one reason I feel like Alyssa and I have a relatively healthy relationship is we both hold apologies and forgiveness as a non-negotiable. That one will be humble enough to apologize and one will be graceful enough to accept and speak forgiveness.

Think of one thing you maybe haven't apologized for that you said, did or held onto today, yesterday or maybe even long ago. And maybe you can't think of anything but talk about forgiveness with your wife or girlfriend and chat about how you can integrate it more into your relationship or do better at it.

JOURNAL BELOW:

WRITE WHAT YOU LEARNED TODAY, HOW IT
WENT AND WHAT MEMORIES WERE MADE.

_____

_____

_____

_____

_____

_____

_____

_____

_____

_____

_____

_____

_____

_____

DAY SEVEN: MUSIC

Alyssa and I both came of age or were teenagers at the end of the 90's and beginning of the 2000's. Because of this, we were in the glory days for music playlists. Back then a playlist wasn't just something you made really quick on your iPhone but it was actually incredibly thought out and structured. You then burned it onto a CD for your significant other. (Please tell me I'm not the only one remembering this right now.)

Now, I don't want to be the person that is always like, "Well, back in MY DAY," that is classic dad syndrome. But there was something special that has been lost about the making of music mixes we'd gift to each other. I, to this day, still remember a few different ones I made Alyssa while we were dating and even one I made during our break-up that I gave to her after we got back together.

Whether it's an iPhone playlist or a CD you burn, make her a playlist today. Be thoughtful with the theme. Either songs that remind you of her, that tell your story from the beginning or songs that you hope represent your relationship.

JOURNAL BELOW:

WRITE WHAT YOU LEARNED TODAY, HOW IT WENT AND WHAT MEMORIES WERE MADE.

DAY EIGHT: SWITCH

Alyssa and I have a pretty good rhythm in the home. You know-who takes out the trash normally, who does the grocery shopping and more. For example, I'm the kitchen cleaner upper. Why? Because I'm a little OCD about organization. (I'm that guy that likes vacuuming the carpet because of the lines it makes after you're done.) So that means I do the dishes, wipe down the counters, put the leftover food away, etc. And Alyssa is in charge of grocery shopping and meal planning. Now, of course, neither of these are so rigid we can't each jump in and help each other out once in awhile. But normally we do the things we've learned mesh well with our relationship.

Today, think on one thing that is her "normal" responsibility that you can do to surprise her. This could be making the bed, doing the shopping, taking the trash out, feeding the dog, etc. For the dating couples reading this, you probably have to get a little more creative since you aren't in the same home to be able to have a ton of different opportunities.

JOURNAL BELOW:

WRITE WHAT YOU LEARNED TODAY, HOW IT WENT AND WHAT MEMORIES WERE MADE.

_____

_____

_____

_____

DAY NINE: NOTES

Sticky notes are the best thing ever. They are good for to-do lists, daily reminders, pranking a friend by putting them all over their car (or is that just me). Words are a powerful thing. They can build up, they can tear down. Something about each new day brings the need for a new set of encouraging words. Alyssa and I do this a million different ways but it can be me telling her things I enjoy about her or it can be her leaving sticky notes around the house with things she appreciates about me.

So think of the top 10 traits or qualities you love about her. Write them down on separate pieces of paper. Then put them all over any place she normally would see them in a day. For example-the nightstand, the place where she gets coffee in the cupboard, her speedometer in her car, etc.

JOURNAL BELOW:

WRITE WHAT YOU LEARNED TODAY, HOW IT WENT AND WHAT MEMORIES WERE MADE.

_____

_____

_____

_____

_____

_____

DAY TEN: STORIES

Stories are powerful. Whether we realize it or not, we think in story. We are not mindless computers absorbing data. We give that data flesh. The data gets humanized. It gets storied. And a lot of times, story is the very way we remember our past and look towards the future. As a couple, we know this is true. We don't see our relationships as random abstract things but instead the crazy story of how two lives intersected and never were the same again.

I mean, if you've been together for any length of time, you know getting asked your story is something you almost begin to memorize. The cookie cutter version. I realized the other day, that every time I tell the story of Alyssa and I, I feel this little spark of joy and gratitude that I ended up with her. There's something about recounting your story that gives your relationship strength. The good, the bad, the easy, the hard, the breakup, the kids, the first date or that awkward first kiss. (Which Alyssa and I definitely had. That's a story for another time though.)

Whether it's when the kids get put down or a coffee date in the morning, go back over your story today. There's always more to learn and hear, so try to ask questions or things you maybe have never heard. Talk about the hard times so far. Talk about the good times so far. Then the most fun part, I think, is talk about when you do this again in, say, 10 years, what do you want your story to be then? What does the next 10 years look like?

JOURNAL BELOW:

WRITE WHAT YOU LEARNED TODAY, HOW IT
WENT AND WHAT MEMORIES WERE MADE.

DAY ELEVEN: FACEBOOK

I actually remember Facebook stalking Alyssa before I had ever met her. She was a girl who had caught my eye from a mutual friend and so I'd go on her page and scroll through pictures. It took awhile but I finally got the courage to write her a message on there. This was back in 2009 and I can still go into my facebook and see it today.

The fun part about the internet is it leaves a lasting trail (or the bad part about it too). It's like a time capsule. So go in and message your girl with a sweet, romantic note. And if you don't have Facebook, get creative. Write her an email, leave an Instagram comment, etc.

JOURNAL BELOW:

WRITE WHAT YOU LEARNED TODAY, HOW IT WENT AND WHAT MEMORIES WERE MADE.

DAY TWELVE: FOOD

I love food. Like, seriously, love food. For example, I have a minor obsession with Chipotle...that guac though! Food is something that actually really ties together mine and Alyssa's relationship. We both believe in eating good food, having good meals, while enjoying good conversation. Food is almost the scrapbook for all our adventures the past four years. We remember most adventures and trips by where we ate and what restaurant was the best.

If you are like most everyone else, you eat around 3 meals per day. Breakfast, lunch and dinner. Sadly one of the things we've lost in our culture is to make food more about efficiency or worship. We either worship the food (i.e. we are tempted to have a poor relationship with food by not stewarding it well and taking care of our bodies) or we see it as nutrients only (we calorie count, we do the math, etc). When food is neither. It's an incredible beautiful gift from our Creator that actually has the beautiful blessing of being a natural relationship builder. It's why most of us feel slightly weird eating alone. I'll be honest though, I'm pretty introverted and like a solo meal, just like I like going to the movies alone too, but I digress. Food is an opportunity to sit at the table, look eye to eye and build relationships. You laugh, cry, love and grow at the table. And not to mention how much fun it is to cook before the food even gets to the table.

Use food to your advantage today. Use food in a way that builds your relationship. That could mean cooking a meal for her. That could mean taking her out to her favorite restaurant. It could mean both of you purposely trying something unique you never have tried, just to have fun. Whatever it is, use food for what it is today-an easy opportunity get grow closer with the person across the table.

JOURNAL BELOW:

WRITE WHAT YOU LEARNED TODAY, HOW IT
WENT AND WHAT MEMORIES WERE MADE.

DAY THIRTEEN: HER WORLD

I absolutely love *Back To The Future*. It's my favorite movie of all time. In my office I have a *Back To The Future* poster, Marty and Doc figurines, as well a now discontinued Deloran Lego set. To say I'm a fan, is an understatement. In fact, I always know other fans based on my constant use of one liners from the film. ("There's that word again, heavy. Is there something wrong with the earth's gravitational pull in the future?") I know they *aren't* a fan if I drop a line and they just stare blankly.

When I got married, I wanted to see if my wife was a BTTF fan too but to my surprise, she hadn't seen the movie yet. We ended up watching it on our honeymoon. I remember watching it with Alyssa and being able to tell she thought it was fun and good movie, but didn't think it was life changing, like I did. If my memory serves me correctly, we've even watched it since then. Alyssa isn't a huge fan but keeps watching it. Why? Because she wants to enter into my world. She wants to know the one liners so she can use them with me. She wants to watch the movie because she wants to get just that much closer with me.

Entering into the world of your wife or girlfriend is vital to a healthy relationship. It always saddens me when I see a couple and it's very much a "he does his thing, she does her thing" type of relationship. Good and fun relationships enter into each other's spaces. How can you enter her world today? Maybe that means there is something she likes you can research a bit before dinner, so you can have a fun conversation with her about it while you eat. Or maybe it means you can you go get a pedicure with her. This one really isn't all that bad even though us guys hate on it. Someone cleaning my feet, making them look good and then ending it all with a foot massage-fine by me!

JOURNAL BELOW:

WRITE WHAT YOU LEARNED TODAY, HOW IT
WENT AND WHAT MEMORIES WERE MADE.

DAY FOURTEEN: DREAMS

Alyssa and I were only dating at the time but I remember when she started to mention how she was looking to find a new hobby. Photography was something she mentioned as one of those possible hobbies. So I filed that away and waited. Waited to see if any of those listed bubbled back up. And again photography did. She mentioned how she really wanted to start getting into it but didn't have a camera. The problem is I was broke and couldn't buy her a camera. She had a good steady job though and soon enough, bought a camera. A few months went by and she started to get really into it but didn't have that good of a lens.

I started saving. I had some photography friends I'd text and message asking them what good lenses were. Finally I bought a lens and surprised her with it. What's awesome is she's been able to take pictures of families, high schoolers and more with that camera.

See, in a relationship both of the people will have dreams, hopes and future plans. Either a skill they wish they had or something they've been saving up for for awhile and the list goes on and on. Maybe she wants to get better at cooking. Maybe she wants to learn the guitar. If you can think back on recurring themes on the past few months or years of your relationship-what would one be that she wants to do but hasn't gone for it yet?

Whatever that answer is, today do something towards that. That could mean buying her a cookbook or finding free YouTube videos on cooking. Then maybe write out a card or note about how much you love to see her chase her passions and dreams and how you're her biggest cheerleader.

JOURNAL BELOW:

WRITE WHAT YOU LEARNED TODAY, HOW IT
WENT AND WHAT MEMORIES WERE MADE.

_____

_____

_____

_____

_____

_____

_____

_____

_____

_____

_____

_____

DAY FIFTEEN: SERVING

One of the best pieces of advice Alyssa and I ever got about marriage was to always remember that it's about giving, not taking. Or another way to put it is: marriage is about serving, not about getting served.

Think how much that latter one is true, even though we probably wouldn't admit it aloud. We structure our days, say certain things and do certain things in hopes that we would get served or that we would get what we want. Secretly, if our girlfriend or wife doesn't do those things we start to get resentful or contemptuous. We start having that inner dialogue of, *"She should....if only she....I can't believe she expects me to always..."*

One of the biggest joys of life is to get to serve your wife or girlfriend. Service is actually secretly the key to joy. The reason I say secret is because most people haven't discovered that. Sure it takes a little bit more time and energy and sure, sometimes it feels harder than being served. Not many people, once done doing something for someone, thinks, "Wow! Well that was a total waste." No. We realize it did something in us. It created joy, not only in us, but the person we served.

Do one act of service today for your girlfriend or wife. For me, this usually means I make the bed, give her a back rub or give the kiddos a bath. Whatever it is, serve her and then tell her how much of a joy it is to serve her.

JOURNAL BELOW:

WRITE WHAT YOU LEARNED TODAY, HOW IT
WENT AND WHAT MEMORIES WERE MADE.

_____

_____

_____

_____

_____

_____

_____

_____

_____

_____

_____

_____

DAY SIXTEEN: LISTEN

By nature, I'm a fixer. I like to tinker with things, take them apart, put them back together. When something doesn't go the way I planned, I start analyzing it and wondering *how I can fix it.* This is a good trait most of the time (you know, when I'm building something or trying to solve a problem). But if I'm not careful, this can be hurtful to Alyssa.

Whenever she is feeling down, something bad happened or she just needs to talk, the last thing she wants me to do is try and fix it. In fact, she'll literally even say in some of our discussions, don't try to fix it, just *listen.* Now of course I'm just trying to be helpful when I try to solve the problem but I'm trying to be helpful on my terms, not hers.

To truly love someone, you love them on their terms. Meaning you offer encouragement, blessing, love, kind words, etc. in a way that they best receive, not the way you best receive. For Alyssa and most but not all girls, listening is huge. They want to feel listened to. Heard. Seen. (Shoot, this isn't just a girl thing because I guess I'm that way too. It's natural to desire just to feel understood.)

So how can you listen better today? Make a special point to not talk as fast. Ask double the amount of questions you usually do. Or say "Can you tell me more about that?" or "Why do you like that or feel that way, etc?"

JOURNAL BELOW:

WRITE WHAT YOU LEARNED TODAY, HOW IT
WENT AND WHAT MEMORIES WERE MADE.

DAY SEVENTEEN: CHANGE

"Consider how tough it is to change yourself and you'll understand what little chance you have in trying to change others." -Jacob M. Braude

If that above quote isn't a smack to the face, I don't know what is. In a relationship, once the butterflies and such start wearing off, you start to notice things. Things that start to annoy you, bother you, frustrate you and upset you about the other person (and they certainly start to notice those things about you). One of the temptations is to want to change the person. You think *if only they would change this one thing, life would be a lot easier or better.* And while that might be the case, you'll realize your efforts are probably futile.

Trying to change the other person for your benefit in a relationship only brings more hurt, pain and heartache. Now don't get me wrong, change is good and both of you will change over time, but Alyssa and I have both noticed that's best done through prayer and the Holy Spirit. Instead of Alyssa or I telling each other about something we think needs to change, we start praying for that person and ask God to either A) show them the area they need to change or B) show ourselves where maybe we have area for growth. It might be harder but better than trying to change them.

Think on one thing that you usually want to change about your wife or girlfriend. Now really dig deep and ask in what ways could you actually change on that issue? For example, I hate making the bed and Alyssa loves to make the bed. We fought about it off and on for a year in our marriage. I tried so hard to change her. And finally God convicted me and said if she wanted it made, then I should serve and love her in that way. So now it gets made every morning and I haven't brought it up since.

JOURNAL BELOW:

WRITE WHAT YOU LEARNED TODAY, HOW IT
WENT AND WHAT MEMORIES WERE MADE.

DAY EIGHT-TEEN: COMPLI-MENTS

Words are an interesting thing. They have immense power. Compliments are one of those things. I've noticed lately though that compliments have different levels of power based on who is giving it. A stranger might compliment me and I'm encouraged but when Alyssa compliments me it does so much more. Why? Because I'm closest to Alyssa and she's the love of my life. When the person who loves you and knows you still compliments you, that has power.

Robert Brault once said, "There is no effect more disproportionate to its cause than the happiness bestowed by a small compliment." Isn't that so true? It's the easiest thing to do, yet can bring such an enormous amount of blessing to a person. And Mark Twain even said, "I can live for two months on a good compliment." Words give life. They encourage and build up.

So not only give intentional compliments to your wife or girlfriend today, but go one step further. Every time you give her a compliment, write it down on your phone or a piece of paper. Then at the end of the day give her the paper or a note with all of the compliments on it to show her how much you care about her and spoke life to her today.

JOURNAL BELOW:

WRITE WHAT YOU LEARNED TODAY, HOW IT WENT AND WHAT MEMORIES WERE MADE.

_____

_____

_____

DAY NINE-
TEEN:
HARD-
SHIPS

Harriet Ann Jacobs was famous for saying, "There are no bonds so strong as those which are formed by suffering together." If someone were to ask me what things Alyssa and I have gone through in marriage that made us grow the most or strengthened our marriage-it'd no doubt be the hard things. Relationships, financial things, tough news we got from a friend, etc. Every time it's hard walking through it but looking back there is something special about hardships that actually act as a glue when walked through together.

Of course that doesn't mean we should be going hunting for hardships. It also doesn't mean we should avoid them. So many times in relationships we try to do everything in our power to take the easiest road, make the easiest decision or do whatever will cause the least amount of tension or toughness.

What if instead of dreading those moments, we instead embraced them? What if we didn't search them out but when they landed on our doorstep, we welcomed them? As moments to grow together in a way that prosperity or success never could.

Today, reflect on a hardship you and your wife or girlfriend have gone through in your relationship. Talk about how it grew you together and what you learned from it.

JOURNAL BELOW:

WRITE WHAT YOU LEARNED TODAY, HOW IT
WENT AND WHAT MEMORIES WERE MADE.

_____

_____

_____

_____

_____

_____

_____

_____

_____

_____

_____

_____

DAY TWENTY: WASH FEET

I still remember the day I proposed to Alyssa. I had my two friends go before us to this secluded beach where they'd set the scene before we got there. They put out rose petals, lit candles and hung up pictures from our relationship lining the pathway down from the car to the beach.

And when I got down to the bottom, there was a blanket and a bottle of champagne. It's hard for me to remember every little detail because it was such a blur (and I was so nervous). One thing I do remember is that before I proposed, I got down on my knees, took out a thermos of warm water and a washcloth from my backpack and began to wash her feet. I then proceeded to tell her I wanted this to be a symbol of our relationship, of me serving her and lifting her up in every regard...and then I asked her to marry me.

There's something about foot washing that is incredibly humbling. It feels a little awkward, yet holy. It's been a picture for thousands of years of service, originating in antiquity where foot washing was more of a necessity in many desert climates. While it might not be functionally as needed, it's still just as powerful of a picture to show care and affection.

Wash her feet today. Feel free to make it special by writing a little letter you read to her or setting up a picnic for her after. Ultimately though, let her know how much you care and how you enjoy serving her.

JOURNAL BELOW:

WRITE WHAT YOU LEARNED TODAY, HOW IT
WENT AND WHAT MEMORIES WERE MADE.

DAY TWENTY-ONE: CAMP OUT

I was in love with making forts as a kid. I'd get all the sheets, pillows, chairs and anything else I could use around the house to build these intricate forts right in the middle of the living room. My mom wasn't always a huge fan (for the simple fact the whole house looked a tornado went through it) but she let me do it nonetheless.

There's something about making a fort that creates this fun sense of adventure and imagination. In fact, that's one thing I think we are sorely lacking these days, especially in romantic relationships. Imagination is no longer a thing celebrated for your whole life. Creativity is no longer a muscle we routinely work out. Both of these things are seen as traits to be left in childhood.

What if I told you creativity, adventure and imagination is sometimes the key to a fun and healthy relationship? Thinking outside of the box, mixing it up every once in awhile and doing things you wouldn't normally do helps jumpstart a relationship.

Today built a fort with her. Make it as elaborate or simple as you want. That's the fun part. You get to be a kid again and there's no judge after you're done building. Laugh along the way and work together. And when it's done, hangout inside of it and tell stories.

JOURNAL BELOW:

WRITE WHAT YOU LEARNED TODAY, HOW IT
WENT AND WHAT MEMORIES WERE MADE.

_____

_____

_____

_____

_____

_____

_____

_____

_____

_____

_____

DAY TWENTY-TWO: THE WALK

One of Alyssa's favorite things is to go for a walk. She usually goes every day, whether to just get out or get a good workout. To her, if she doesn't go for a walk she feels a little pent up or closed in being inside all day. I personally am not a huge fan of walks. I am more so now then before but for awhile I pretty much hated them. I didn't like doing any physical activity that wasn't also fun at the same time (basketball, swimming, etc).

I've started to change a little and now go with Alyssa on a lot of those walks. You know what's funny? There's something about walks that just renew your energy and spirit for the day. Also the conversations are always good. It's strange but there's some things that just make for better conversations than others (like sitting high up on a water tower, going for a walk, etc).

There are things we've talked about during our walks that have helped reset our focus that week. Or bring new energy and life to our relationship that week. Or it's just the pause needed to get a sense on how we are doing as a couple.

Today, go for a walk. Could be around the neighborhood or you could drive somewhere and then walk. Doesn't have to be big. Just walk, chat, hangout and relax.

JOURNAL BELOW:

WRITE WHAT YOU LEARNED TODAY, HOW IT
WENT AND WHAT MEMORIES WERE MADE.

_____

_____

_____

_____

_____

_____

_____

_____

_____

_____

_____

_____

DAY TWENTY-THREE: KINDNESS

When you first start dating, you're on your best behavior. You do things and say things to impress but also shower kindness on her. For example, it's common gentlemen etiquette to open the door for her, pull out her chair, bring flowers and more.

For some reason if you've been dating or married for any length of time, this stuff starts to wane. It starts to fade and no longer happens. But shouldn't it be the opposite? If the love and connection is growing, shouldn't that stuff at least stay the same or grow as well?

I know for me, I get really comfortable with Alyssa thinking, "Oh, she knows how much I love her." That then makes me complacent. She does know that but active pursuit is different than complacency. One leads to a flourishing relationship and one doesn't.

Today, ask yourself what you can bring back that you did when you were dating. What small gesture can you continually do as an encouragement to her? Maybe that means open the door for her again, bring her flowers or compliment her.

JOURNAL BELOW:

WRITE WHAT YOU LEARNED TODAY, HOW IT
WENT AND WHAT MEMORIES WERE MADE.

DAY TWENTY-FOUR: CHEESY PICK-UP LINES

I'm a big fan of cheesiness. I'm the king of bad jokes and I love the most ridiculous pick-up lines. Just ask Alyssa. At this point she just barely laughs and makes a face that somewhat communicates, "Man, I sure got lucky marrying this guy."

My favorite thing to do is to surprise her with pick-up lines or bad jokes all throughout the day, especially when she leasts expects it. We haven't even gotten out of bed and I'll say, "Do you have a band-aid? Because I scraped my knee falling for you."

There's something about them that just bring a joy and spontaneity to our relationship that is really fun. It makes her laugh and when you can make your wife or girlfriend laugh, you know there's nothing better.

The task for today is hop on Google and find 10 of your favorite cheesy pick-up lines. Then spread them out throughout the day. You can tell them to her, write them down or text them to her. Watch out! She will probably fall in love with you all over again!

JOURNAL BELOW:

WRITE WHAT YOU LEARNED TODAY, HOW IT WENT AND WHAT MEMORIES WERE MADE.

_____

_____

_____

_____

DAY TWENTY-FIVE: THANK-FULNESS

I once heard a quote that basically said, "It's not happy people who are thankful, it's thankful people who are happy." I couldn't agree more. Most don't realize that thankfulness is actually the secret to joy. The reason I call it a secret is it seems many haven't caught on yet! In the Bible thankfulness is elevated almost to the place of being the heart of worship. A thankful heart is exactly what God is looking for and pleased in. When we are thankful it brings Him glory and us joy. In fact, the Bible even says that thankfulness is the will of God! (1 Thessalonians 5:18). A lot of times we think the will of God is this mystical thing like what joy we are to take or what passion we should pursue- when the Bible says just being thankful is His will.

I've seen this to be true in my relationship with Alyssa. I'm serving her the best, loving her the best and being fulfilled the most in our relationship when I'm thankful and on the hunt for things to be thankful for.

That's the task for today. If you have an iPhone or a little sketch pad, go on the hunt for things you are thankful for In her and about her throughout the day and write every one down. Feel free to even mark the littlest things. By the end of the day you should have dozens of reasons, if not hundreds! Dwell on the list that night or maybe even show her all the reasons you are thankful for her.

JOURNAL BELOW:

WRITE WHAT YOU LEARNED TODAY, HOW IT
WENT AND WHAT MEMORIES WERE MADE.

DAY TWENTY-SIX: TIME CAPSULE LETTER

There's something about a handwritten note that just seems a little more thoughtful and memorable sometimes. You could say the same thing in a letter that you could in a text and it'd feel more tangible and worth saving.

In fact, Alyssa to this day still has all the letters I wrote to her over the years. Some dating back 7 or so years. I even used to spray my cologne on some of the letters when we were dating long distance so when she opened the envelope it'd smell a little like me. I know, I know, my game was on point at that stage in my life. Thank goodness we didn't start dating in middle school or else those letters would smell like Axe body spray (AKA middle school boy's locker room forever).

Letters have a way of even making you, the writer, think things through or say things a little differently.

A letter received in the mail is definitely the most exciting. This is hard though when you are married because you live in the same house. This is why today's challenge is a fun one.

For today, write her a letter. Then get two envelopes and two stamps. Mail the letter to a friend or a parent who can hold onto it for a little bit. Then after a few months or weeks have them put the letter in the other second envelope addressed to her and mail back her. This way she receives a letter months later from you.

JOURNAL BELOW:

WRITE WHAT YOU LEARNED TODAY, HOW IT
WENT AND WHAT MEMORIES WERE MADE.

DAY TWENTY-SEVEN: WEEKLY JOURNAL

One of my favorite things Alyssa and I do every week is we get away for about an hour and go through what we call our "marriage journal." Alyssa's parents watch the kiddos and we head off to the beach or somewhere restful and go through the journal. It's a journal we keep that has 5-7 questions we ask ourselves every week and then record the answers in there. It's really changed the whole dynamic of our relationship in regards to us communicating well, squashing certain things before they turn big and understand more about each other. Also, it's fun to have a written record of your relationship and how you are doing in different seasons.

We got the idea and questions from a friend and have loved doing it ever since. The cool part is you have full control over it to make it different or the same. The questions we ask are:

1) What brought you joy this week?
2) What's something that was hard this week?
3) What's one specific thing I can do for you this week?
4) How can I pray for you this week?
5) Is there anything that's gone unsaid this week?
6) What's a dream or thought that's been on the forefront of your mind this week?

And then once a month we ask ourselves how our finances and sex life are doing. In all honesty, it's been life changing for us to do this journal. I get to hear how Alyssa's week has been hard when maybe before I wasn't paying attention all that well. Also I get to hear how I can serve her in the week ahead.

Today find some journal around the house or go get a brand new one. Game plan how you and her are going to do your relationship journal and either keep or edit the questions we ask. Commit to getting away or spending one hour together on it every week.

JOURNAL BELOW:

WRITE WHAT YOU LEARNED TODAY, HOW IT
WENT AND WHAT MEMORIES WERE MADE.

_____

_____

_____

_____

_____

_____

_____

_____

_____

_____

_____

_____

_____

_____

DAY TWENTY-EIGHT
MAKE IT KNOWN

One of the cool things about the internet is it gives you a perspective on things being bigger than just you. I've found, seen or been a part of some of the coolest little communities online. They have encouraged one another, helped each other financially and built things for under privileged folks around the world. Sometimes the internet gets a bad rap but I think it's at its strongest when a community is coming together in a way they couldn't have offline since they are all across the world.

Now I'm not a huge fan of the person who pretty much does social media PDA (you know what I'm talking about, unless maybe that's you). You know, that old friend that posts pictures of him and his wife or girlfriend making out every other picture. It's like, bro, take that offline.

But there is a space for treating your platform online as a natural extension of your life offline. And if there is someone you love and care about in real life, it makes sense that would show up online sometimes. So for today, write 3 things you are thankful for or recount your story in the picture caption. Post a picture of her and you lifting her up with encouraging words. Use the hashtag #31creativeways so that folks can see the power of a community that believes in relationships and lifting each other up!

JOURNAL BELOW:

WRITE WHAT YOU LEARNED TODAY, HOW IT WENT AND WHAT MEMORIES WERE MADE.

DAY TWENTY-NINE: SCRIP-TURE

The Scriptures are such a powerful thing. They are active, living and God's very own word. They can breathe life into a relationship when that relationship comes under the beauty of it.

For Alyssa and I, scripture is everything. Both of us try to read at least a few minutes each day (even though with two young kids that is a tough task). It anchors our relationship and reminds us of what's important and what matters. Ultimately the better I follow Jesus, the better I can serve my wife. And the more I drift from Jesus, the more I realize I'm not loving and serving my wife well.

A marriage or relationship that prioritizes the scriptures as a center point for them and their relationship is one that will flourish.

Today find a scripture passage that you want to dwell on for the next month in regards to your relationship. It can be a verse you want to remind yourself of in order to serve her better or it can be one you both agree on as your "relationship verse" for the next month.

JOURNAL BELOW:

WRITE WHAT YOU LEARNED TODAY, HOW IT WENT AND WHAT MEMORIES WERE MADE.

_____

_____

_____

_____

DAY THIRTY: HER CAR

You can tell a lot by a looking inside a person's car. If you looked inside of mine you'd realize I have two kids (two car seats), I'm not *that* clean and I like a good clean air freshener. The car to a lot of people is a second home or space, since they use it every day to get around, get to work, run errands and more.

I still remember to this day both mine and Alyssa's cars when we were dating. Oh, how many memories those cars hold. Us going on our first dates, many late night drives to get food and of course our epic listening sessions of old Disney songs or N'Sync throwbacks where I blew a speaker in mine.

Today the challenge is to do something with the car that serves her. That could mean washing her car. It could mean vacuuming the inside of the car. Or it could mean simply leaving little notes all around the car (the dash board, the glovebox, under the seat, in the trunk).

JOURNAL BELOW:

WRITE WHAT YOU LEARNED TODAY, HOW IT WENT AND WHAT MEMORIES WERE MADE.

_____

_____

_____

_____

DAY THIRTY-ONE: PRANK HER

Light hearted pranks can make an amazing memory. It might just be my personality but I've always been a huge fan. For example: one of my favorites was when I put my friend's car on Craigslist with a super cheap price and he basically got a phone call every 2-3 minutes for a week straight. Or little things like trying to scare Alyssa when she comes around the corner.

Pranks, if done right, have a way of creating a little fun moment and memory for people. A fun one if they have an iPhone is you can screen capture their home screen, make that picture the new background picture, and put all the apps on the second page so now it looks like she has a frozen home screen. Another one is you can also put a toy spider or snake somewhere in the cupboard (actually, if she is anything like Alyssa she will HATE this one).

Basically doing something harmless, fun and creates no damage. Do something that you think will make her laugh. And who knows, you just might start a little couple prank war!

JOURNAL BELOW:

WRITE WHAT YOU LEARNED TODAY, HOW IT WENT AND WHAT MEMORIES WERE MADE.

DAY THIRTY-TWO: YOUR TURN

You didn't think there was going to be a day 32 did ya? We thought we'd add one more day, to turn it over to you. Think of any idea, any gesture, or any kind thing you can do for your significant other today. Be creative. Be loving. And most of all show them how much you care. Also, we'd love to hear what you picked for day 32! We might even end up including it in future versions or volumes of this book. You can upload your idea at *upload.31creativeways.com*. We can't wait to hear how creative you guys are and what y'all came up with!

JOURNAL BELOW:

WRITE WHAT YOU LEARNED TODAY, HOW IT WENT AND WHAT MEMORIES WERE MADE.

_____

_____

_____

_____

_____

_____

_____

A NOTE FROM US AFTER FINISHING THIS BOOK.

First off, you all rock! For reals. Complete rockstars. Why? Because you care about your relationship. You're investing in it. You believe in it. It matters to you.

We believe that a relationship is like a garden. For it to flourish it needs proper nourishment, constant care, awareness of the things trying to hurt it and sometimes is a little messy. This book is just a start to hopefully continuing or taking that leap of putting you and your significant other on the path to a vibrant and beautiful relationship.

So thank you for doing this journey with us. Thank you for reading this book. And thank you for just being you. We'd love to hear from you and how the challenge went by sharing something online with the hashtag #31creativeways. We are constantly on that hashtag to see all the awesome stuff you guys are doing, ways you tweaked one of our challenges to make it better and to see all the fun you're having!

OTHER RE-SOURCES

For those who maybe are getting this as a gift or don't know much about us, below are just a few other things we have created and done over the past few years. We hope they encourage you!

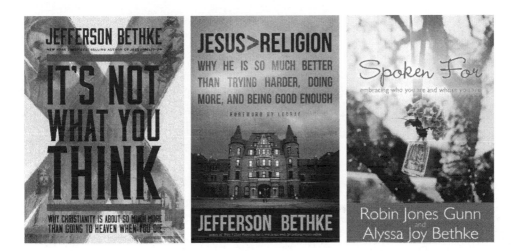

Find at
JEFFBETHKE.COM

Find at
BETHKEWORKSHOPS.COM

WHERE
TO FIND
US
ONLINE.

We love when folks give us a shout on social media,
so feel free to stop by and say hey!
Would love to e-meet you.

 INSTAGRAM

@jeffersonbethke
@alyssajoybethke

 TWITTER

@jeffersonbethke
@alyssajoybethke

 FACEBOOK

fb.com/jeffersonbethkepage
fb.com/alyssajoybethke

 SNAPCHAT

jeffersonbethke

 WEBSITES

jeffbethke.com
alyssajoy.me
bethkeworkshops.com
31creativeways.com

We are always looking for great things to help marriages and relationships. We've found a few we absolutely love and hope you guys will too!

DATEBOX:

We LOVE this. It's a subscription service that sends you a fully curated Datebox every month to your doorstep. For example, during the Christmas season in December we got a box that included a gingerbread making kit, two custom mugs, hot cocoa mix, a Christmas playlist and bunch more goodies. We have a blast every time one shows up on our door. We wanted to hook you guys up to check it out. If you use code 'bethke' at checkout at http://www.getdatebox.com, you get your first month 50% off. Definitely a steal of a deal and something we love!

STRONGERMARRIAGES.COM:

This is a phenomenal website that just has crazy amounts of content to help and build any marriage out there! They have courses, blogs, books and more. It's a site that isn't afraid to talk about real life either, which is so important to us.

Printed in Great Britain
by Amazon